THE NATIONAL POETRY SERIES

The National Poetry Series was established in 1978 to publish five collections of poetry annually through five participating publishers. The manuscripts are selected by five poets of national reputation. Publication is funded by The Exxon Corporation, The Ford Foundation, Friends of the National Poetry Series, James A. Michener, The Mobil Foundation, The National Endowment for the Arts, Edward J. Piszek, and the five publishers—E. P. Dutton, Graywolf Press, William Morrow and Company, Persea Books, and The University of Illinois Press.

The National Poetry Series, 1985

Living Gloves
  Lynn Doyle
  Selected by Cynthia Macdonald/E. P. Dutton
Local Time
  Stephen Dunn
  Selected by Dave Smith/William Morrow and Company
Palladium
  Alice Fulton
  Selected by Mark Strand/University of Illinois Press
Saints
  Reginald Gibbons
  Selected by Roland Flint/Persea Books
As Long As You're Happy
  Jack Myers
  Selected by Seamus Heaney/Graywolf Press

LOCAL TIME

LOCAL TIME

STEPHEN DUNN

William Morrow and Company, Inc.
New York

Grateful acknowledgment is made to the editors of the following
magazines in which these poems first appeared:

Antaeus, "Toward the Verrazano"; *The Bennington Review,* "Natural";
Crazyhorse, "Local Time"; *The Georgia Review,* "He/She"; *Kansas
Quarterly,* "Skin Diving"; *The Missouri Review,* "Insomnia"; *New England
Review/Bread Loaf Quarterly,* "Living with Hornets," "Round Trip,"
reprinted by permission from *New England Review,* copyright © 1983,
1985 by Stephen Dunn; *Painted Bride Quarterly,* "Aubade"; *The Paris
Review,* "Among Men"; *Poetry,* "Aerial in the Pines," "All That We
Have," "Ignorance," "Sleeping with Ghosts"; *Poetry Northwest,* "At the
Smithville Methodist Church," "Halves," "The Obscene," "The
Return"; *Prairie Schooner,* "Just Fascinated," "Long Term," "Money for
the Dead," "On the Greyhound," reprinted from *Prairie Schooner* by
permission of University of Nebraska Press, copyright © 1986 by the
University of Nebraska Press; *Quarterly West,* "Accident in the Snow on
the Way to Amadeus," "After the Argument"; *raccoon,* "Leaning
Toward Grandfather"; *The Seneca Review,* "From Underneath," "Letter
Home," "The Substitute," "Two Women"; *Tendril,* "Topless Bar;
Texas, First Time" first appeared in *Tendril* magazine.

Library of Congress Cataloging-in-Publication Data

Dunn, Stephen.
  Local time.

  I. Title.
PS3554.U49L58   1986   811'.54   85-21619
ISBN 0-688-06153-2
ISBN 0-688-06296-2 (Quill: pbk.)

Printed in the United States of America

First Edition

1 2 3 4 5 6 7 8 9 10

BOOK DESIGN BY JAYE ZIMET

to Dennis and Carolyn

ACKNOWLEDGMENTS

My thanks to the John Simon Guggenheim Memorial Foundation for its support. And to the corporation of Yaddo for two residencies, which led to the completion of this book. My thanks also to Stockton State College for two summer grants.

CONTENTS

3 LOCAL TIME

ONE

ROUND TRIP

ROUND TRIP

I watched the prairie repeat itself
    until it got beautiful, the geometry
      of farms, the flatness

that made interesting the slightest
    undulation. Never had the sky
      touched so far down.

Then, because mood invents landscape,
    the flatness turned irredeemable,
      I felt it go on and on—

something lush and vacant in me
    wished for an edge again,
      a city, an ocean.

I returned east, began to revise
    my childhood, wanted women
      with sharp tongues,

my evening walks shadowy and open
    to possibility. And because the mind
      gets what it wants

but rarely the way it wants it,
    I got mugged on a streetcorner,
      fear brought home in a real cold sweat

on a real November evening,
   and city life began to insist—
      like jazz, like dream—

it would be nothing but what it was.
   In a rented cabin up north,
      Christmas vacation,

I closed the door and gave whatever in me
   wanted to be alone and pitied
      its hard uncomfortable chair.

But after a while the light
   I didn't believe in
      shone in anyway through the windows,

the walls I had pulled in
   closer and closer
      returned to their proper places.

One day I opened the door
   and it wasn't quite overcast,
      little pieces of sun

reached the tip of my shoe,
   and it was as if I'd touched a breast
      for the first time

and touched it and touched it
   until, having touched it enough,
      I finally saw the blue veins . . .

2

Ever since, I've been trying to build
 a house of cards amid a house
  of people, hard edges and angles,

each one overlapping. From the beginning
 I've been careful of the one
  that would be too many.

I've kept out of drafts, house-winds.
 The unexpected opening
  of a door, an indelicate voice,

these are the hazards of building
 amid people, amid their enthusiasms
  and secret needs

to destroy. One should be alone
 to build a house of cards.
  One should have a hardwood table,

perfectly flat. One should have none
 of the clutter that comes
  from living a life.

That's why, though, I've been trying
 to build a house of cards
  in a house of people—

to do what's difficult to do
 and so be pleased
  with each card I add,

each moment short of collapse.

3

There's been a cricket in the livingroom,
   a male because only the male
      is built to sing

or to produce what passes for song.
   It's a mating call, that high sound
      that comes from rubbing

forewing against forewing, plaintive,
   like someone scared blowing
      a little whistle in the dark.

Day and night it's been making that sound
   from somewhere in the room.
      I've opened drawers,

I've pulled chairs away from the wall,
   ready with two paper cups
      to catch it

and take it outside. It came in, I suppose,
   in a confusion of warmth,
      doomed to sing

its song to those who wouldn't understand.
   Now the song grows
      more faint—

why care? it's the end of summer
   and crickets die and come back
      in great, anonymous force.

I'm pulling back the rug, listening
   for what it withholds
      when anyone gets close.

4

Where does the dark come from?
—The dark comes from the weakness
of the infinity of numbers.
        —Andrea Dunn, age 10

How to leave and come back—the schoolbus
    instructs my daughter it's easy
        and that for now is good.

She's off again into numbers, words,
    all the necessary confusions.
        History, she believes,

is what happens to others. Biology is what
    she lives with, but hasn't had.
        I'm watching from the window,

the father who knows education
    is all about departures, who knows
        when things are right

nobody comes home the same. The schoolbus
    has left a hole in the landscape.
        Air fills it now, the low sky

we don't call sky for some reason.
    How to paint a landscape where children
        once played? Swirls and smudges?

My daughter knows where the dark comes from
    and I believe her. She's growing breasts.
        She closes the door to her room.

I'd paint the trees blue because the low sky
    is in them. I'd paint the area white
        where she once did a cartwheel,

maybe with a hint of yellow in it
   for the schoolbus. Off to the side
      lots of red seemingly out of control

yet orderly, like wildflowers.

     5
Nothing's happening but the wind,
   the ferry rocking its way
      toward Delaware, and Delaware Bay

full of big tankers
   at anchor, seemingly poised.
      It's two hours across,

a talk to give, one night
   away, then two hours back,
      the kind of minor traveling

which tests nothing at home, nothing in self.
   "Travel is the saddest pleasure,"
      a friend once said. He meant

all those hours that exist
   outside of work and play and love.
      The boredom of sailors

must be enormous, as great as the boredom
   of those on land who hope for weather
      to change their lives.

We're bored too, the few of us
   making this trip, off-season, the spectre
      of necessity

evident in how we sit and stare.
    Later, I'm thinking, each of us
        will have a story to tell

about the bay and the ships.
    We'll leave out all we can,
        all that is a traveler's life

or a sailor's life. We'll make our friends
    wish they were us, we'll replace experience
        with what we say.

      6
This is one of those stories,
    Minnesota to New Jersey,
        a return home

in search of home, regular departures
    to find the limits
        of home—

impulses finding reasons, words.

The great decisions that change
    a life—hardly decisions
        at all; a wild hunch

or avoidance, the unknown agent x
    coursing through the body
        like a bastard gene.

I'm only sure that collapse
    waits just beyond
        standing still,

the next complacency. Even now,
   my day off, I'm thinking
      I'll get in my car,

get out of here, no rhyme except
   internal rhyme, the clicks
      and bells that go off

when the body has heard itself
   and acted. I know where
      I'll go—

ball-field, casino, deserted beach—
   some not-home place
      where I can pivot

at supper time, make my way back
   as if I'd made a choice.

      7

Last week at this time
   Canada geese flapping overhead,
      heading south:

impossible to warn them of hunters
   up since dawn. A few hours later
      three separate phone calls

told me the same person was dead.
   By the third my voice
      had nothing in it;

it was days before the letting go.
   I watched the jays in the yard
      chasing smaller birds,

taking all the seed for themselves. That's where
   the dark comes from, I thought,
      some weakness in the motive

or of the heart, a bunch of jays
   exercising their muscle, and *poof*,
      nothing's left but jays.

I should have called the dead man's wife.
   I should have reread his poems,
      made him a good ghost

and myself sorrow's perfectly correct man.
   I put on my running shoes,
      ran the full circle

of the park, showered, turned on the
   important game. The whole season
      was on the line,

the announcer said, and it was.
   In a nearby room the noise of others—
      a child's whine, my wife saying No—

mixed with my noise to form
   the familiar. For a while
      nothing tumbled down.

HALVES

Once again after dawn before questions
   arrange themselves
into what to do, who to see, and each of us

is most pleasurably alone—the first sounds
   of traffic, muffled
by trees, find their way to the ear;

we don't know what we're hearing, and don't
   care. The light
touches us. We turn toward the dark.

Soon the equally mysterious world of women
   and men, of momentary
common agreement and wild misunderstanding,

will impose itself naturally on the simplest event.
   Anatomy will send
its differing messages to syntax and sense,

and beyond sense—among the senses—
   unbuttoned women
will witness grown men become babies again

and later watch their mouths shape perfectly
   controlled sentences
from distances laughable and immense.

In the morning, though, now, while the secret
     intercoms in our dream rooms
are still open and each separate body knows

but does not reach for what it wants,
     we all live in the same
country, share the same absurd flag.

We keep our eyes closed as long as we can,
     hang on to the vestiges
of night as if we were balancing

two delicate and always vanishing halves.
     Then the alarm, and the body rises
to yearn for what is here and gone.

HE/SHE

Brought up never getting punched
    in the mouth for saying more
        than the situation can bear,

she argues beyond winning,
    screams indictments
        after the final indictment

has skewered him into silence,
    if not agreement.
        The words she uses

mean she is feeling something large
    which needs words, perhaps
        the way Pollack needed paint.

Next day the words are unimportant
    to her, while all
        he's thinking about

are the words she used—
    if recovering from them
        is possible.

Years ago, the schoolyard taught him
    one word too many meant
        broken fingers, missing teeth;

ι

you chose carefully, or you chose war.
    You were the last word
        you let live.

She was in the elsewhere girls were,
    learning other lessons,
        the ones men learn

too late or not at all; you took in,
    cared for, without keeping score
        you shaped a living space

into a kind of seriousness.
    Retract those words, he says.
        But she is only

sensing his reserve, his inability
    to perceive that her wrong words
        meant so much hurt and love.

AFTER THE ARGUMENT

Whoever spoke first would lose something,
   that was the stupid
      unspoken rule.

The stillness would be a clamor, a capo
   on a nerve. He'd stare
      out the window,

she'd put away dishes, anything
   for some noise. They'd sleep
      in different rooms.

The trick was to speak as if you hadn't
   spoken, a comment
      so incidental

it wouldn't be counted as speech.
   Or to touch while passing,
      an accident

of clothing, billowy sleeve against
   rolled-up cuff. They couldn't
      stand hating

each other for more than one day.
   Each knew this, each knew
      the other's body

would begin to lean, the voice yearn
    for the familiar confluence
        of breath and syllable.

When? Who first? It was Yalta, always
    on some level the future,
        the next time.

                    This time

there was a cardinal on the bird feeder;
    one of them was shameless enough
        to say so, the other pleased

to agree. And their sex was a knot
    untying itself, a prolonged
        coming loose.

HONOR

Because in any relationship the wrongs accumulate,
  because each of us has the goods,
    the bad goods, on the other—

how to leave closed the historical wound
  when a new argument begins, how,
    when anger reaches

back into its arsenal, to come forward
  with, if not a rose,
    then at least

the knife that's never been used,
  which shines a little
    as it does its terrible work.

LONG TERM

On this they were in agreement:
everything that can happen between two people
happens after a while

or has been thought about so hard
there's almost no difference
between desire and deed.

Each day they stayed together, therefore,
was a day of forgiveness, tacit,
no reason to say the words.

It was easy to forgive, so much harder
to be forgiven. The forgiven had to agree
to eat dust in the house of the noble

and both knew this couldn't go on for long.
The forgiven would need to rise;
the forgiver need to remember the cruelty

in being correct.
Which is why, except in crises,
they spoke about the garden,

what happened at work,
the little ailments and aches
their familiar bodies separately felt.

AMONG MEN

Yesterday in the locker room
a young man told his friend
how he did it to her
and what she did to him.

He wanted all of us
to hear as if the act weren't complete
until it was repeated among men.
Her diminishment, his power—

one of the old stories.
He and his friend were naked.
They had just played
with a shared ferocity

within four walls, without rancor.
It had been terrific, they kept saying.

THE GULF

He knows how dangerous it is for a man

to speak of it, but it's his subject too,
    it enters his life
monthly like a bill from an old creditor

who sometimes overcharges. His need to speak
    of it, quietly, out loud,
without jokes, reaches back to his first girl,

the first sudden change of mood and the apology
    that never came,
the first time someone was late, *late*, a word

with the future in it. Oh, discomfort hates
    a distant calm voice
and what she can't bear is the discomfort

he's never experienced, how the absence of it
    makes him ignorant, stolid.
If he could, if he were the saint

she wants him to be after an outburst
    takes him by surprise,
he would swallow her words, walk away,

he would immediately understand it was her body,
    not her,
which was responsible. But he is no saint,

he's failed her when nothing was breaking
    inside him.
Why should she think a good reason

makes bad behavior any more tolerable?
    He thinks like a man,
he can hear her saying to women

who know exactly what she means. He doesn't
    understand. He'll never understand.

JUST FASCINATED

Animals, even plants, lie to each other
all the time. . . . What is it that enables
certain flowers to resemble nubile
insects, or opossums to play dead . . .
what about those animals that make
their livings by deception, the
biological mimics, the pretenders. . . ?
                    —Lewis Thomas

There was so much to lie about,
so many advantages to changing
a story, rearranging an afternoon,
that to tell the truth
was un-Darwinian, destructive
as having no fear.
                    This is what
he told her, trying to be as honest
as he could.
                    Weren't people
happier when they had something
to believe, when the confusions
of truth could be smoothed away?
How natural to behave
like an opossum, a chameleon,
the fox with good reasons
setting another false trail.

She listened to him, amused
he had picked such small animals

as examples. Honesty was what
she couldn't help, as unchosen
as a blush. Her face was a public
radar screen, even now
it was registering disdain.

Lying as seldom as he had
over the years
was an accomplishment.
Besides, he added, honesty is the lie
that always reveals . . .

She was smart enough to know
all such discussions, on some level,
were about sex,
that this had little to do
with the nuances of lies or truth.
Tell me what you're really talking about,
she said.

He was just fascinated
with how natural it was,
even some plants do it, he said,
it's all, these mysteries
of the physical world, so interesting.

THE SHAME PLACE

After he did what he did, and was ashamed,
    he went into himself
where shame makes its poor home

and lived there amid the excessive heat,
    the Dead End signs.
Shame was his rent and he paid in shame

until it was spent and he returned
    to his public body
which was waiting like a debtor

to apologize. He never felt so clean.
    At work,
where it was expensive to be ashamed,

he wished everyone could visit
    their shame place,
could live for a while without credit

or esteem. He felt sorry for everyone
    unchanged.
But there was no hope for the shameless

with their profit charts and perfect reasons.
    And what could he say
to the beaten who had lived too long

eating their hearts and words?
    Their shame places
were hovels, all the energy shut off.

Soon he lied again, hurt someone, rekindled
    what never burns to ash.
Once again his shame place opened and took

him in. It had carpets. A plush chair
    covered the spot
where he had sat and writhed.

LETTER HOME

For L.

Last night during a thunderstorm,
awakened and half-awake,
I wanted to climb into bed
on my mother's side, be told
everything's all right—
the mother-lie which gives us power
to make it true.
Then I realized she was dead,
that you're the one I sleep with
and rely on, and I wanted you.
The thunder brought what thunder brings.
I lay there, trembling,
thinking what perfect sense we make
of each other when we're afraid
or half-asleep or alone.

Later the sky was all stars,
the obvious ones and those
you need to look at a little sideways
until they offer themselves.
I wanted to see them all—
wanted too much, you'd say—
like this desire to float
between the egg and the grave,
unaccountable, neither lost nor found,

then wanting the comfortable
orthodoxies of home.

I grew up thinking home was a place
you left with a bat
in your hands; you came back dirty
or something was wrong.
Only bad girls were allowed
to roam as often or as far.
Shall we admit
that because of our bodies
your story can never be mine,
mine never yours?
That where and when they intersect
is the greatest intimacy we'll ever have?

Every minute or so a mockingbird
delivers its repertoire.
Here's my blood
in the gray remains of a mosquito.
I know I'm just another slug
in the yard, but that's not what
my body knows.
The boy must die is the lesson
hardest learned.
I'll be home soon. Will you understand
if not forgive
that I expect to be loved
beyond deserving, as always?

        Saratoga, 1984

INSOMNIA

What should be counted was counted
up to a hundred and back.

And sleep came by, I think,
sensed too much movement and left.

Now there's desire meeting absence,
the multiplication of zero,

the mind, as always, holding out
for a perfect convergence

like a diver entering water
without a splash. There's a part

of me terribly stilled and alert,
a silence that won't shut off.

And there's this need to put on the light,
to not sleep on sleep's terms, sleep

which is after all like you, love,
elsewhere and difficult.

THE NIGHT THE CHILDREN WERE AWAY

When she comes home he's waiting for her
    on the secluded deck, naked,
        the wine open,

her favorite cheese already sliced.
    Though he hasn't done anything
        like this in years

he knows she'll laugh at his nakedness
    as one laughs at seeing
        an old friend

at a dirty movie. Then she'll take off
    her clothes, join him.
        Tonight

he wants to make love profanely
    as if the profane
        were the only way

to disturb, to waken, the sacred.
    But neither is in a hurry.
        They sip wine,

touch a little, nothing much needs
    to be said. That glacial
        intolerable drift

toward quietude and habit, he was worried
    that he'd stopped worrying
        about it.

It's time, a kiss says, to stop time
    by owning it, transforming it
        into body-time, hip-sway

and heartbeat, though really the kiss says
    now, the now he trusts
        is both history

and this instant, reflexive, the good past
    brought forward in a rush.

ALL THAT WE HAVE

To John Jay Osborn, Jr.

It's on ordinary days, isn't it,
   when they happen,
those silent slippages,

a man mowing the lawn, a woman
   reading a magazine,
each thinking it can't go on like this,

then the raking, the turning
   of a page.
The art of letting pass

what must not be spoken, the art
   of tirade, explosion,
are the marital arts, and we

their poor practitioners, are never
   more than apprentices.
At night in bed the day visits us,

happily or otherwise. In the morning
   the words good morning
have a history of tones; pray to say them

evenly. It's so easy, those moments
    when affection is what
the hand and voice naturally coordinate.

But it's that little invisible cloud
    in the livingroom,
floating like boredom, it's the odor

of disappointment mixing with
    kitchen smells,
which ask of us all that we have.

The man coming in now
    to the woman.
The woman going out to the man.

TWO

STORIES

PARABLE OF THE FICTIONIST

He wanted to own his own past,
be able to manage it
more than it managed him.
He wanted all the unfair
advantages of the charmed.
He selected his childhood,
told only those stories
that mixed loneliness with
rebellion, a boy's locked heart
with the wildness
allowed inside a playing field.
And after he invented himself
and those he wished to know him
knew him as he wished to be known,
he turned toward the world
with the world that was within him
and shapes resulted, versions,
enlargements.
In his leisure he invented women,
then spoke to them about
his inventions, the wish just
slightly ahead of the truth,
making it possible.
All around him he heard
the unforgivable stories
of the sincere, the boring,
and knew his way was righteous,

though in the evenings, alone
with the world he'd created,
he sometimes longed
for what he'd dare not alter,
or couldn't, something immutable
or so lovely he might be changed
by it, nameless but with a name
he feared waits until you're worthy,
then chooses you.

STORIES

It was back when we used to listen to stories,
    our minds developing
pictures as we were taken into the elsewhere

of our experience or to the forbidden
    or under the sea.
Television was wrestling, Milton Berle,

Believe It Or Not. We knelt before it
    like natives
in front of something sent by parachute,

but when grandfather said "I'll tell you a story,"
    we stopped with pleasure,
sat crosslegged next to the fireplace, waited.

He'd sip gin and hold us, his voice
    the extra truth
beyond what we believed without question.

When grandfather died and changed
    what an evening meant,
it was 1954. After supper we went

to the television, innocents in a magic land
    getting more innocent,
a thousand years away from Oswald and the shock,

the end of our enormous childhood.
   We sat still
for anything, laughed when anyone slipped

or lisped or got hit with a pie. We said
   to our friends
"What the hey?" and punched them in the arms.

The television had arrived, and was coming.
   Throughout the country
all the grandfathers were dying,

giving their reluctant permission, like Indians.

AT THE SMITHVILLE METHODIST CHURCH

It was supposed to be Arts & Crafts for a week,
but when she came home
with the "Jesus Saves" button, we knew what art
was up, what ancient craft.

She liked her little friends. She liked the songs
they sang when they weren't
twisting and folding paper into dolls.
What could be so bad?

Jesus had been a good man, and putting faith
in good men was what
we had to do to stay this side of cynicism,
that other sadness.

O.K., we said. One week. But when she came home
singing "Jesus loves me,
the Bible tells me so," it was time to talk.
Could we say Jesus

doesn't love you? Could I tell her the Bible
is a great book certain people use
to make you feel bad? We sent her back
without a word.

It had been so long since we believed, so long
since we needed Jesus

as our nemesis and friend, that we thought he was
sufficiently dead,

that our children would think of him like Lincoln
or Thomas Jefferson.
Soon it became clear to us: you can't teach disbelief
to a child,

only wonderful stories, and we hadn't a story
nearly as good.
On parents' night there were the Arts & Crafts
all spread out

like appetizers. Then we took our seats
in the church
and the children sang a song about the Ark,
and Hallelujah

and one in which they had to jump up and down
for Jesus.
I can't remember ever feeling so uncertain
about what's comic, what's serious.

Evolution is magical but devoid of heroes.
You can't say to your child
"Evolution loves you." The story stinks
of extinction and nothing

exciting happens for centuries. I didn't have
a wonderful story for my child
and she was beaming. All the way home in the car
she sang the songs,

occasionally standing up for Jesus.
There was nothing to do
but drive, ride it out, sing along
in silence.

ACCIDENT IN THE SNOW ON THE WAY TO AMADEUS

When we went into that spin on the turnpike
   the calm I felt
was pure lucidity—a sense of what was close

and couldn't stop, endless variations
   amid snow-
covered cars; everything white, open.

We'd been doing forty, a speed I'd recommend
   for spinning
on a deserted frozen lake where joy

is feeling powerless, yet safe. The guard rail
   stopped us. I think
we hit it twice, rocked, but didn't flip,

came to rest pointed toward the city
   and *Amadeus*.
Soon we'd be considering mere excellence

versus genius, God's unfair handling
   of genes and gifts.
But for us God was good, or away and unjust

some other place. No longer in control
   or under that illusion,
we drove toward Manhattan like dreamers

in a race for who could go slowest
    in a slow world.
In the play, Mozart is a brilliant fool,

proof of nothing. Salieri a man we've met
    or have been, corrupt,
his work a small pleasure for everyone.

I was happy to be a witness, still for a while
    and moved. Outside
the storm was neither better nor worse.

The streetlights were invisible, though their light
    illuminated the snow,
seemed almost to bring it down.

SKIN DIVING

Cadiz, 1967

The rich girls walked arm in arm, untouchable,
    big silver crucifixes
below their necks, while the men
    in outdoor cafés

smacked their lips at peasant girls too poor
    to forget their bodies.
Each night my blond wife and I would go out
    for shrimp and baby eels

or sherry and langostinas, and the men
    turned and turned,
whispered, made gestures.
    At Carnival—

amid the floats carried by penitents,
    the noise and the crowds—
a furtive touching, Spanish boys pressing
    into what they couldn't have.

Sundays it all exploded; the bulls dipped
    into the horses, the matadors
into the bulls, then the streets filled again
    with a wild vicariousness.

One day after El Cordobés had frightened
    and aroused us,
putting his ear to the tip of a bull's horn,
    a Spanish friend taught me

how to skin dive for moray eels.
    You had to anger them
so they'd come at you, shoot the spear
    straight down

their throats after the huge mouths opened.
    I had no desire
to do such a thing, but I went down anyway
    and later watched him

walk the streets with a moray around his neck,
    smiling, proud, terribly hurt
when my wife stepped back, wouldn't take it,
    his gift, in her hands.

LEANING TOWARD GRANDFATHER

When I get overtired from too much
   this or that,
or the natural random accidents
   occur too close

to home, I begin to see myself keeping
   the family tradition alive
by death, one of those stupid early deaths
   that makes a mockery

of will, of what we will or won't.
   Last summer my sail broke
on the Northumberland Strait. The sky said
   storm. All I had

was a lighter for a signal and the memory
   of a story grandfather used to tell—
how he was saved at nightfall; a fisherman's
   tale, but true.

I flicked the lighter on and off.
   Nobody existed anywhere
in the world. Come morning, I was dangling
   my feet over the side,

having a smoke. The storm had passed;
   I was close to shore.

I'd like to say it was a grand adventure,
   surviving without being saved.

I'd like to think history, through luck,
   always can be revised.
But in our family we follow our hearts.
   They lead us into still waters,

they break. We have to learn how to live fast,
   grandfather said before he died.

ON THE GREYHOUND

On the Greyhound from Paducah
to Memphis, a blond woman
asks the driver to stop
so she can call her little boy.
"He may be kinda worried
since his father got all burnt up
in a fire last week and died."
Against the rules we stop
at the Down Home Diner,
wait while the boy is assured
his mother's coming home.
"It was my ex-husband," she says to us,
"so I didn't care, but the boy
kinda worries, you know."
None of us knows, but we hear
and the bus starts up again,
taking us deeper into the foreign
country our country can be.
The landscape is autumn-pale.
Hog farms and white-
shingled houses, billboards
as we're approaching a big town.
If the blond woman were traveling
the Jersey Turnpike, smokestacks
and absence of life
suggestive of some final error,
no doubt she'd wonder
where am I, what caused this.

No doubt someone on that bus
would be talking to himself,
more crazy than different,
too lost in his own world
to be considered regional.
We pass Ripley and Hopewell,
Glimp, Mumford.
The woman is silent now.
All this is familiar to her;
she just wants to get home
to her little boy.
Just outside of Memphis,
a man sitting across from her
leans her way, says "You know,
during Elvis Death Week this year
I never saw it so crowded."
And they talk about the weeping
and from how far the people came.

TWO WOMEN

This time I wasn't looking to look.
I was waiting for a friend
and for all I chose to see
the park could have been an immense
desolate beach. A wedding party
was taking place near the fountain.
I noticed it at first, heard it,
but I was tired of celebrations
not mine. I had turned away.
Blue sky. The disciplined world of light.
To my left was a small building—
a power house—and two young women
from the wedding party had come
to pee behind it. They didn't see me.
It was the redness of their dresses
that caught my eye. They pulled down
their panty-hose, squatted in unison,
all the while talking. It was like
watching Degas's ballerinas
resting languidly at a rehearsal.
I was careful not to move,
careful to keep the scene
as I wished to remember it.
Because by now it had become mine
and I saw their wrist corsages
and that one's dress was ruffled
where the other's was plain.

Fifteen seconds? Sixteen? They must
have drunk the same amount of champagne,
raised the glasses to their lips
at exactly the same time.
I think it was Appolinaire who said
it's necessary to see, to drink,
to piss as well as crickets
in order to sing like them.
Two women practicing to be crickets!
I was sorry to see it all end,
the hitching up of the panty-hose,
then each of them touching their hair
out of habit as if the air were a mirror
and beauty something conscious again.
They returned to the party.
My friend arrived.
The rest of the day was bright yellows,
greens, every little thing coming out
of its hiding place to be seen.

THE SUBSTITUTE

When the substitute asked my eighth-grade daughter
    to read out loud,
she read in cockney, an accent she'd mastered

listening to rock music. Her classmates laughed
    of course, and she kept on,
straightfaced, until the merciful bell.

Thus began the week my daughter learned
    it takes more than style
to be successfully disobedient.

Next day her regular teacher didn't return;
    she had to do it again.
She was from Liverpool, her parents worked

in a mill, had sent her to America to live
    with relatives.
At night she read about England, looked at her map

to place and remember exactly where she lived.
    Soon her classmates
became used to it—just a titter from Robert

who'd laugh at anything. Friday morning,
    exhausted from learning
the manners and industry of modern England,

she had a stomachache, her ears hurt, there were
    pains, she said,
all over. We pointed her toward the door.

She left bent over like a charwoman, but near
    the end of the driveway
we saw her right herself, become the girl

who had to be another girl, a substitute
    of sorts,
in it now for the duration.

THE OBSCENE

The year my father made friends
   with the obscene caller
was the year Royal Vacuum let him go.

Aunt Claire had a breast removed.
   McCarthy began to paint
the country a garish red, and I, helpless

before God, studied my catechism dreaming
   of the short curly hair
Mary Ellis showed me between her legs.

The call would come after midnight.
   Father hung up at first,
told my mother with the bad heart

"wrong number," but the calls didn't stop.
   Once, he threatened the man,
then screamed all the forbidden words.

A few days later, though, he delayed
   going to bed, waited
by the downstairs phone. We heard him

speaking in hushed, confidential tones.
   "Mind your own business,"
he said when we asked. "Leave me alone."

Mornings he'd hawk the employment agencies.
  Something was cooking,
something was in the fire.

Our dinners became strained, silent.
  No one expected him
to prepare for bed; he'd make sure

his cigarettes were near the phone.
  One night the call
that punctuated our nights didn't come.

Never came again. My father found work.
  In the spring,
on a day so warm that girls wore

nothing on their arms, I was confirmed.

COCKTAIL WAITRESS: ATLANTIC CITY

Every man I meet wears gold chains,
flashes big bills at the tables,

gives me a fake address, an alias.
Years ago I could take a few Quaaludes

and kill the loneliness with sex,
but now as soon as they speak

I want to be home alone.
I'm getting old. It's gotten so

if I believe anything a man says
I give him three points. If he doesn't

say "nigger" within the first hour
of conversation I give him three more.

I'm thinking of going day shift,
would you believe it, Steve?

Different class of guys, maybe.
But I don't know if I could stand

the nights if no one calls.
Days you can shop, walk the streets,

but at night loneliness is different.
On my night off I try to write,

sometimes go so far into myself
I think there's no getting out.

That poem I gave you about the girl
who disappears in her own room,

did you know, Steve, who she was,
that it wasn't creative writing at all?

TOPLESS BAR; TEXAS, FIRST TIME

She was graceful
and lewd,
the strobe lights

added circles to what was
already rounded
and what was rounded

moved for everyone
beyond intimacy and claim.
When my friend approached

she shook her breasts,
tilted herself
his way, let him dream.

And when he held out
a dollar bill, slipping it
under her G-string,

the exchange seemed fair,
understood; each according
to his or her needs.

I was thinking
how all that's sexual is crude
from a distance,

but I was *thinking*,
enjoying myself far less than he.
Then I felt that old independence

between my legs, my penis on its own
rising halfway,
a middle place, no place

stupider for a man to be.

FROM UNDERNEATH

A giant sea turtle saved the life
of a 52 year old woman lost at sea
for two days after a shipwreck
in the Southern Philippines. She rode
on the turtle's back.
        —*Syracuse* Post-Standard

When her arms were no longer
strong enough to tread water
it came up beneath her, hard
and immense, and she thought
this is how death comes,
something large between your legs
and then the plunge.
She dived off instinctively,
but it got beneath her again
and when she realized what it was
she soiled herself, held on.

God would have sent something winged,
she thought. *This* came from beneath,
a piece of hell that killed a turtle
on the way and took its shape.
How many hours passed?
She didn't know, but it was night
and the waves were higher.
The thing swam easily in the dark.

She swooned into sleep.
When she woke it was morning,

the sea calm, her strange raft
still moving. She noticed the elaborate
pattern of its shell, map-like,
the leathery neck and head
as if she'd come up behind
an old longshoreman
in a hard-backed chair.
She wanted and was afraid to touch
the head—one finger
just above the eyes—
the way she could touch her cat
and make it hers.
The more it swam a steady course
the more she spoke to it
the jibberish of the lost.
And then the laughter
located at the bottom
of oneself, unstoppable.

The call went from sailor to sailor
on the fishing boat: A woman
riding an "oil drum"
off the starboard side.
But the turtle was already swimming
toward the prow
with its hysterical, foreign cargo
and when it came up alongside
it stopped
until she could be hoisted off.
Then it circled three times
and went down.
The woman was beyond all language,
the captain reported;
the crew was afraid of her
for a long, long time.

MONEY FOR THE DEAD

For Christine Martens

She believed in her money
the way I believe in poems
that arise out of dim light
and fill vacancies hardly known.
It was square, mostly orange,
the designs vaguely Chinese
though indescribable as if
only the dead might understand.
When she gave it to me—
large bills, medium, small—
I thought: something instead of flowers
for my parents' graves,
a prodigal boost for their souls.
But that was a secular man's fancy.
The money was art, nothing less.
I put it on the wall

above my desk, and believed
the little I could: that if we carry
our dead forward
as we carry our pasts,
then the dead will be pleased
each time I look up.
Oh, it's a lot to believe.
Most days I see thin parchment,

strange calligraphy,
and know my parents are beyond
help, beyond pleasure, awakened
in me for a moment, put to rest again.

THE RETURN

It's taken years to stop the voices
    of the dead
from rising up. Subdued now,

they're content to be on call.
    My father
and Melville and Dostoyevsky—

always complicating the afternoon.
    My mother insisting
with Carlisle on an Everlasting Yea

and I needing to debunk, destroy.
    They've let me go,
and so the true embrace begins.

How to say father and be small
    and mean it again.

THREE

LOCAL TIME

SLEEPING WITH GHOSTS

The ghosts who've resided for years
in those perfectly made beds
in houses you visit overnight

were once just guests like you
or true inhabitants who died
quietly, almost happy, with the lights out.

They are the ghosts who let you sleep,
who speak, if they speak at all,
into the ear closest to the pillow,

offer you assurances of dawn
while their vaguely palpable bodies
touch you like a strange wind

looking for a place to rest
beneath the covers.
Those other ghosts, wronged

and forever in league with wrong,
so much has been said about them.
But the ghosts who sleep with you

and let you sleep are the ones
you might have invited to your bed
had you known them in proper time.

They might have believed in the future
even then, and would have let you
leave them easily, knowing somehow

it would come to this, you one day
drifting toward them, without fear,
in a world wholly theirs.

TOWARD THE VERRAZANO

Up from South Jersey and the low persistent
pines, pollution curls into the sky
like dark cast-off ribbons
and the part of us that's pure camera,
that loves funnel clouds and blood
on a white dress, is satisfied.
At mile 127, no trace of a tree now,
nothing but concrete and high tension
wires, we hook toward the Outerbridge
past Arthur Kill Road where garbage trucks
work the largest landfill in the world.
The windscreens are littered, gorgeous
with rotogravure sections, torn love
letters, mauve once-used tissues. The gulls
dip down like addicts, rise like angels.
Soon we're in traffic, row houses, a college
we've never heard of stark as an asylum.
In the distance there it is, the crown
of this back way in, immense, silvery,
and in no time we're suspended
out over the Narrows by a logic linked
to faith, so accustomed to the miraculous
we hardly speak, and when we do
it's with those words found on picture postcards
from polite friends with nothing to say.

GRAY

I've seen him there, and been him,
    someone who's gone
to the ocean to walk everything off,

hood up, hands gloved, a gray man
    on a gray coast
in, say, March. I've seen him pause

where there's no division between
    retreat and advance,
watched him examine the dead

horseshoe crabs and what the gulls
    have picked clean.
If his dog is with him, he talks

to his dog. If he talks to himself
    it's because what he needs
to say should not be overheard.

I've seen him stare at waves as if
    expecting change.
I've seen the smile that means

he's caught himself staring, has finally
    seen the negative
of himself in all its conspicuous gray.

Then his sadness breaks like a fever
    and he becomes
a man alone unable to stop

laugh after rising laugh, not quite
    dangerous, yet
hardly ready for the long drive home.

IGNORANCE

The ancient dream of flying has come true
and I look up, unamazed.
Why doesn't it fall?
A child's question I can't explain.
I dress my ignorance in what I know.
Once there were pterodactyls, I say.
Once the sky was guesswork and birds.

It's immense and small, so high
it isn't making a sound.
If it were to drop bombs, if by luck
a few of us were saved
and had to start again, I'd have nothing
for the pain but words.

I tell my daughter
I've been up there, in the sky,
but both of us are unimpressed.
She's seen *Star Wars*. And I no longer
ask for a window seat.
Faced with flying, I think of death.
I will not tell her this

as I will not tell her the house
is her cave and I the hairy man who returns
each night, often speechless and confused.

THE IMMENSE BLUE BOWL

He woke up into his one and only life,
   allowing himself
the sweet penalties of sensing, knowing.
   The second hand

on the clock: an extension of his breathing.
   Daylight:
an immense blue bowl for him to measure.
   Death was in the house,

as always. This was one of those mornings
   when he felt it nearby,
maybe because the night before had been
   so good, maybe because

he hadn't felt any pressure lately
   and something in him
that needs pressure wanted to value again
   the world.

At breakfast even the oatmeal seemed a gift;
   the oranges,
a gift from a genius. Later, he taught a novel
   as if the right word

placed here, not there, was magic.
   The students rose

to meet him; two drifted above him
    near the ceiling.

The rest of the day he searched the faces
    of colleagues, passersby,
like someone soul-poor turned loose
    in a human Lost & Found:

dim-lit eyes, mouths turned down
    at the corners.
He would fondle everyone, speak to them
    of Death

until their chakras opened, use his tongue
    as a key
to what was dormant, forgotten, unlived.
    This went on

until evening, flowers turning his way
    as he passed,
small animals pressing against his legs.
    It wasn't that it ended,

his body just gave in to the old
    protective intelligence
which engenders sleep, though he was far
    from sleep.

His shoulders drooped happily.
    He sat down
to the unbearable news of the world
    and there was Death,

omnipotent and careless, exercising
    its brilliance.

It was a force he still could celebrate
    if men

weren't its agents, if the murderer
    were only a concept,
the arsonist not so contorted
    with vengeance.

He poured himself a drink, let his hand   .
    for comfort
slip lazily into his pants,
    sure that nothing

he'd do would contradict anything else.
    In his notebook that evening
he wrote the one word "bittersweet," after which
    he put a colon.

COMPLETION

After the floor was grooved and tongued,
the walls paneled, windows framed,
a sadness came over him,
a wild sadness he did not resist.
It was close to elation
as if something melting in his shoulders
had reached his chest.
He wanted to dance.
He wanted to dial a neglected friend.
This was his room. Everything in it
he had wedged, fitted, nailed.
Outside, in the street and beyond,
was the world made by others,
fascinating, not to be trusted.
Always it had called him
and always he came.
His room seemed foolish, an umbrella
in a typhoon. It was done.
It certainly wouldn't do.
The sadness was all over him now.
He'd have a party, a bon voyage.
He could see himself breaking
a bottle on the hard, pitchpine floor.
Instead, he looked out the window.
He thought: the goddamn grass,
the goddamn leaves. A blue Toyota
passed. A red Dodge. It seemed comic
how much didn't belong to him.

When his wife returned from work
he said: Look, it's finished,
but he knew the room meant nothing
to her. His books would go in it,
his desk. Did his wife belong to him?
Could anyone *belong* to anyone else?
If neglected people weren't so sad
he would've called his neglected friend.
He was ready for that party again.
It would be evening, the indirect lighting
would confirm how careful he'd been
to keep the room peculiarly his.
He imagined his guests asking
about the switchbox. He imagined speaking
about the miter work and joists,
the fluted molding above the door.

LIVING WITH HORNETS

Since June they've been chewing on wood fibers,
   transforming them
      into a papery home

weightless, we suspect, as a Chinese lantern—
   and soon we'll know.
      The air has cooled,

time for the queen to leave the nest
   behind. In a few weeks
      we'll be brave enough

to bring it inside, examine the emptiness
   these papermakers called home.
      Mid-summer, we had to decide

if we could live with hornets. We saw
   the small nest in the evergreen
      next to the garage,

liked its brainy architecture, its mysterious
   growth. We showed each other the book
      that said hornets eat flies.

But we couldn't decide and so did nothing
   or, rather, by doing nothing
      allowed a hornets nest.

By the time our daughter got stung in August
  (for lack of tact
    near the evergreen), the hornets

had so proven themselves good neighbors
  we put a mud pack on her arm,
    calmed her, held back

destruction, that sting for sting.
  They have only one season,
    the hornet book says,

are driven by what they don't understand.
  Their life is paper
    and service, and come October

we'll hold what's left of these truths
  in our hands.
    It's all you finally get,

we've decided, by chancing to live
  with hornets. It's what
    we're waiting for.

NATURAL

I looked for the usual mole or mouse,
　　stunned or half-ripped up.
This time it was a baby bird tossed

or fallen from its nest, no hope for it
　　now, no going back.
But my cat didn't know what to do—

each time he extended his paw, the bird
　　opened its beak
as if asking to be fed.

It was the riskiest strategy a victim
　　could use: praise the gun,
make believe you don't know what it's for.

Only of course it wasn't strategy,
　　but hunger.
Birds that believed themselves wiser

were squawking up above. The cat got bored,
　　tucked himself
into himself, reduced his eyes to slits,

left me with this creature fallen so far
　　from warmth or help.
I had an eye-dropper in the medicine chest,

instruments that could hold and drop
   a worm.
But I'd been thinking of what was natural

all along. The little bird made a sound,
   presented itself
like a pressed leaf come upon in a book;

   surprising, precious,
already living the life of the dead.

UNDER THE BLACK OAKS

Because the mind will defend anything
it has found the body doing,
I tell my family I'm out here
because the house is cold,
because it's Saturday,
because I feel like it.
The rock-hard acorns are falling
and I've placed my chair
where one has just fallen,
the beginnings of a theory . . .
The family points out
there are places I could sit
where nothing but the sun
could hit me,
but of course I know about them.
It's one of those mornings
when there seems so much time to fill,
so many correct ways to fill it,
the tedium of virtuous leisure.
The white sky above the oaks
displays its familiar open mockery.
When the wind comes up
the acorns fall like hailstones.
I sit in my chair
listening to how they brush leaves
on the way down, a natural jazz,
thud and silence, then another thud.

My family shouts "Come in, come in,"
but I'm out under the black oaks
and will not budge.

AUBADE

After Philip Dacey

To rise before the children rise,
before life as it gets lived
has begun, is to rise into the silence
of another time, is to think your children
safe in the half dark dawn,
the fog protective, the short morning
of childhood prolonged.

To start a fire before the children rise,
to open the blinds, break the eggs,
is to act by act
shed the night, the adult night
your children sense
and have slept through once again.

And when it's fully gone,
when all that's risen has moved
into niche or arc, after the wind
comes up, after the traffic starts,
you watch the children (stretching
toward what they must
and must not have) rise without alarm.

AERIAL IN THE PINES

To cut off the top branches
   of the majestic pine
(once unthinkable for us)

was a bit of nature traded
   for clear reception,
for what was fundamental now.

The tree looked foolish, like someone
   well dressed
with a bad haircut, but the television

had become what to do
   with difficult time,
important, an antidote to speaking

if need be, company when our nerves
   couldn't bear the silence
of a printed page. We watched sports,

the human spirit rising
   and falling
against excellence, against time—

one good clear transcendence
   worth one desecration
of a pine—though some nights

we needed what was mindless, too,
   those final chases
ten minutes before the hour

along winding ocean roads, what we expected
   when we expected it
(as if in a dream) coming true.

LOCAL TIME

The trees were oaks and pines.
The unaffordable house

a little bargain with my soul,
a commitment to the dream

my father lost somewhere
between gin and the dotted line.

The siding was cedar.
The weathervane gun-metal gray.

It was odd how dinner hour
was always approaching,

odd how we counted,
what we counted on.

You folded the napkins
in triangles, set the prehistoric

knives and forks. It all seemed
as if it had happened before.

The night came in layers
through the large windows.

When we finished eating
it was wholly there.

The house had double locks
but in the dark a wrong person

would understand: the windows
were made of glass:

the cat wanted out or in,
the cat so easy to impersonate.

We knew that anyone good
would be unafraid of a light

but we turned on the porch light,
left on an inside light

when we went out, advertised
the signs of our presence.

It was what our parents had done
even in a safer time,

it was all their *be carefuls*
awakening inside us

like slow dissolving pills,
messages in the bloodstream.

Anyone good, we were sure,
would be bold enough

to work in the open,
would give the illusion

he could be tracked down,
identified.

Still, we left the lights on,
parents ourselves now,

deterring with conventional wisdom
the conventional criminal—

no defense against the simple
knock on the door, the man

with a mask so perfect
we'd shake his hand.

Whatever time it was
it was local time, our time.

What was foreign never occurred
until we heard it here,

wasn't that true?
And didn't enough happen here?

The retarded girl nearby
swallowed stones.

Schultz stepped off that ledge,
everyone knew,

because his house wasn't home.
It was exactly seven o'clock

when we got the news—
time for us to hear

and not forget the orbital tick
of the planet, the not-

so-merry-go-round. But for us
there was food every day,

clothing for every season.
The work we did left some time

for the work we loved.
To complain was obscene.

To lament the drift of any day
marked us American, spoiled,

believers in happiness,
the capital I.

The wars in small countries were ours
if the world was ours.

Whether the world was ours
we couldn't decide.

Our neighbor said everything sucked.
It all was humungous, he said,

and I knew what he meant.
Oh on certain days,

when the smokescreen of weather
or luck permitted,

we loved the world.
Not to love it, risking nothing,

was to fail only at our desks
sulking over commas and typos

or only in the privacies
of bedroom and kitchen

where we lived largely in miniature.
So we loved the world

when we could. No matter,
our house was a hiding place

and the blood dripped in,
deluged and shamed us.

Where would we go?
To work, to the store,

to the next place on the list?—
as if the next place weren't an alarm

set the night before,
as if there always weren't a dream

to give up, something about to happen
to uncomplicated warmth.

I knew after many hurts
how to hold back

what could hurt me,
how to become hollow, absurd.

Passing churches, I remembered
the old repetitions,

the faked novenas,
but what did I feel, really,

after removing disguise after disguise,
then adding others,

could I know what I felt?
At night the shining

steeple across the lake
was a nuisance or a beacon.

Rocky's all-night bar,
just to the south, was oblivion

or a refuge, often both.
Yet the pleasures were near

like ships just offshore, anchored.
I saw them and peopled them,

heard the music and those ahhs
coming through the air, the walls.

I longed to be a visitor
or the visited, and sometimes I was—

wondering, amid touch and entry,
where the music was

and why intimacy carried with it
such distances.

So many times I lifted
the anchor and let it all go—

in my mind
and from this familiar shore.

I turned further inland
toward bric-a-brac, curios,

the narcosis of purchasing.
I turned toward the skillet,

made something for myself.
But I could sense them,

the replacements coming in—
masted, shapely, moving

through old waters calling to me.
You sensed them, too.

One day, finally daring to speak
of soul, wanting to rescue it

from the unnamed
for my own sake, I decided

it wasn't character
but a candle in the room

of character, visible
around the eyes, the mouth.

It was exciting to discover
I was most aware of it

when it was missing, when nothing lived
or burned behind the eyes

and the voice, a tin box,
couldn't support its words.

Only people wrong for us, I decided,
confused soul

with intelligence or with sorrow.
Discussions with them never touched

down, clicked in. In our true friends
there it was, simply.

It became part of what we meant
when we said their names.

It wasn't enough, of course.
Even in the garden I once

believed spectacular, the tulips
were anybody's pretty girl.

The hyacinths offered such small cheer
I turned to the vegetables

as once I turned to foreign films
for the real.

What could I say?
The garden bloomed

but did not transport?
That I wanted my beauty

a little awkward and odd?
Only the moon flower,

among flowers,
pleased me these days,

lily-like,
opening in the dark.

Every hour the clock struck *now*.
It didn't remind us we would die.

The trees needed to be pruned.
You'd prune the trees.

There was no more milk.
I'd get in the car.

Years ago, when the angels
our parents insisted on

could no longer fly
and our bodies took them in,

it seemed we'd solved by cancellation
how to live on our own.

We bought the house,
the house in the cyclic fog

that looked so new.
It's hours now

since a thunderstorm came,
our little world

of tumult and aftermath
seemingly ratified from above.

Though the sky turned perfect
our dog trembled, hid.

Something was out there,
he was sure. The sparrows,

no less foolish or wise,
returned to the yard and sang.

ABOUT THE AUTHOR

Stephen Dunn is the author of five previous books of poems, most recently *Not Dancing* from Carnegie–Mellon. He holds a Guggenheim Fellowship for 1984–85 and has been awarded two National Endowment for the Arts Creative Writing Fellowships. He teaches at Stockton State College in New Jersey and in the Graduate Creative Writing Program at Columbia. He lives in Port Republic, New Jersey.